An Environment Q&A Book

When Is It Great To Turn Green?

P9-DCT-857

Photo credits:

AP/Wide World Photos—F. Gugliotti: p. 11; Sasa Kralj: p. 27
Archive Photos—Joan Slatkin: p. 7; Hulton Getty: p. 20; Reuters/HO: p. 24; Reuters/Simon Thang: p. 25
DRK Photo—Stephen J. Krasemann: p. 9; Tom & Pat Leeson: p. 12; Stephen G. Maka: p. 15; Larry Ulrich: p. 19; S. Nielsen: p. 20; Andy Rouse: p. 23; John Gerlach: p. 28; Wayne Lynch: p. 29
FPG/International—Arthur Tilley: p. 6; Telegraph Colour Library: pp. 8, 9; Jean Kugler: p. 14; Dennis Galante: p. 16; Scott Markewitz: p. 17; Ed Taylor Studio: p. 21; VCG: p. 22; Bruce Byers: p. 25; David Fleetham: p. 26
International Stock—Jorge Ramirez: p. 10; Willie Holdman: p. 16; Tom Murphy: p. 22; Art Brewer: p. 27
Breck Kent—pp. 9, 23
Tom & Pat Leeson—p. 12
New York Zoological Society—p. 28
Visuals Unlimited, Inc.—Arthur R. Hill: p. 7; D. Clayton: p. 10; Science VU: pp. 12, 20; Glenn M. Oliver: p. 13; Bill Beatty: p. 18; Mark E. Gibson: p. 19; David A. Rintoul: p. 26

Illustration credits:

Cover and all other illustrations—
Justin Ray Thompson

Copyright © 2001
Kidsbooks, Inc.
230 Fifth Avenue
New York, NY 10001

Manufactured in the United States of America

An Environment Q&A Book

When Is It Great To Turn Green?

Written by
Michele Drohan
Caroline M. Levchuck

kidsbooks®
Incorporated

Q. How can pigs clean up a big city?

A. By eating trash! Back in the late 1800s, few poor New Yorkers could afford to have their trash picked up. Instead, they relied on pet pigs to gobble it up! After all, that is what they had done in the European villages where they once lived.

However, not all New Yorkers liked having pigs in the neighborhood. So in 1895, Colonel George E. Waring Jr. was appointed commissioner of street cleaning. He set up New York's first trash-recycling system. Animal waste was collected as fertilizer, and rags and paper were sorted to be reused. Three years later, New York was the cleanest city in the world.

Q. How are landfills like lasagna?

A. Both are created in layers. Lasagna has layers of cheese, sauce, and pasta; landfills have layers of garbage and soil. But that is where the similarity ends.

At one time, people believed that landfills could solve all of Earth's garbage-disposal problems. But now many of these dump sites are almost filled. Another problem with landfills is that the bottom levels don't get much air or sunlight. Because of that, the garbage toward the bottom doesn't decompose very quickly, so it just sits there.

Q. When do plants like leftovers?

A. When the leftovers are in a compost pile. Compost piles are made up of orange rinds, coffee grounds, eggshells, banana peels, leaves, grass, rotten vegetables, and other natural stuff that would otherwise be thrown into a landfill. When you mix these organic leftovers with dirt for a few months, you wind up with great soil.

Besides being ideal for the garden, composting does the planet a world of good. Through composting, garbage that would otherwise wind up in a landfill goes back to the land instead.

Q. What is the lifespan of a garbage bag?

A. That depends. Many garbage bags are made from low-density polyethylene (LDPE), a plastic that is made from the by-products of oil refining. This plastic has a really long life span because it is not biodegradable. In fact, LDPE will *never* break down.

Today, however, new forms of plastic are being developed. There are plastic bags made from cottonseed and cornstarch that will break down over time—some in only six months. These bags are not always available, however, and they are more expensive. As a result, few people use them.

Q. WHAT IS A FOSSIL DOING IN A CAR'S ENGINE?

A. Helping the car run. Just about every automated thing we use today, including cars, ultimately runs on fossil fuels: coal, oil, or natural gas. Fossil fuels started out as plants and animals many, many years ago. Over time, heat and pressure from deep inside Earth turned their remains into coal, oil, and natural gas.

There is a problem with fossil fuels, though. When they burn, they give off carbon dioxide and other gases that, in large doses, harm Earth.

Q. Does radiation cause problems—or solve them?

A. Both. One kind of radiation is the energy sent out by something radioactive, such as the sun or certain elements in nature. This type of radiation can kill living cells, which doctors use to their advantage when trying to kill cancer cells.

One of the biggest problems with some types of radiation, however, is radioactive waste. Nuclear power plants *(right)* use the radiation produced by a nuclear reaction to generate power. The waste products from nuclear power are also radioactive and need to be disposed of carefully to protect living things. Usually, the waste is sealed in special containers and buried. But many people fear that the radiation could leak out and contaminate air, water, or soil.

Q. Could the *sun* light up the world at night?

A. It sure could. Solar energy is quite powerful. In fact, enough sunlight reaches Earth every minute to meet the world's energy demands for a whole year! Solar energy is also clean and renewable. It doesn't pollute the air the way fossil fuels can, and it won't run out anytime soon.

So what are we waiting for? More and more people around the world are switching to solar energy. However, many people still rely heavily on fossil fuels, and switching to solar power can be expensive.

You have probably already seen solar-powered calculators and watches. Other items—such as solar-powered cars *(left)*, homes, and battery chargers—are also available. Maybe your television will be next!

Q. Why are light bulbs real losers?

A. Because most of them are energy-wasting incandescent bulbs *(right)*. These are basically an updated model of the first light bulbs created by Thomas Edison in 1879. Most of the energy from incandescent bulbs is given off as heat. Only a little bit is left to shed light. Luckily, in the 1930s, a much more efficient type of bulb was created: fluorescent tubes. By replacing incandescent bulbs with fluorescent lamps, especially today's super-efficient compact fluorescent lamps *(above)*, people burn a lot less electricity, which saves money and energy.

Q. If a cow burps in Boise, can it raise the temperature in Tahiti?

Buuurp!

A. It's possible. A cow releases about 74 gallons of methane gas daily, mostly through burps. Experts say that methane, along with carbon dioxide and nitrous oxide (collectively known as greenhouse gases) may contribute to a process called the greenhouse effect. As greenhouse gases collect in the atmosphere, they trap the sun's warmth, slowly increasing the temperature on Earth.

Cows are not the only ones releasing greenhouse gases. Emissions from cars and factories give us reason to sweat, too. Although trees and plants help clean the air by taking in carbon dioxide, there are just not enough of them.

Q. Can washing machines help clean the air?

A. The kind that wash clothing can't. But factories have started to install special "washing machines," known as scrubbers, in their smokestacks. These cleaners remove pollutants from smoke before it is released into the air. Thanks to the Clean Air Act of 1970, automakers are also installing special washing machines, called catalytic converters, in car engines. These devices convert the gases in car exhaust to make them less harmful to the air.

Q. How [...] is poll[...]

A. Ve[...]
Mission[...]
world h[...]
junk. W[...]
space sta[...]
need to wa[...]

Traveling[...]
ment. By th[...]
lite reaches[...]
boosters, e[...]
paint chips[...]
junk will bu[...]
atmosphere, this can take many years.
With dozens of rockets launched each
year, that means that there is a lot of junk
left floating around.

Q. How safe are small towns from big-city pollution?

A. Not very. Great big wind belts that circle Earth can carry pollution miles from where it began. This is especially true high up in the air, where there are no trees or houses to block it. So smokestacks in large industrial areas can affect countryside thousands of miles away!

Winds also spread the results of natural disasters, such as wildfires, dust storms, and volcanoes. In 1980, Mount St. Helens (left) erupted in Washington state. Three days later, a volcanic ash cloud had crossed the entire United States. Two weeks later, the cloud had gone all the way around the world!

Q. How is a red wolf like an American alligator?

A. To look at them, you wouldn't think that they are at all alike. One is a reddish mammal, once found throughout the southeastern U.S. The other is a brownish-green reptile, found in the southeastern U.S.

So what do they share? Both were once killed in great numbers in the U.S. Today, both are making a comeback, thanks to the Endangered Species Act of 1973. That law protects plants and animals that are in danger of becoming extinct.

Q. How did dodos get such a bad rap?

A. A lot of people think that dodos were stupid. But the truth is, this now-extinct species was just too trusting. Dodos were spotted by Dutch sailors exploring Mauritius, an island off the coast of Africa, in 1598. That is where dodos lived. At first these birds, which couldn't fly, had no reason to flee. Soon, however, people started hunting them. So did the cats, rats, and pigs that the Dutch settlers owned. The settlers also cut down the island's trees, leaving the dodos unprotected. By 1681, the dodo was gone for good.

A. When the egg belongs to an endangered sea turtle! There are six species of sea turtles on Earth—and all of them are endangered or threatened. Poachers, who take plants, animals, or animal eggs illegally, make it even harder for endangered creatures like sea turtles to survive.

Poachers are out to make big bucks from endangered species, but you can help stop them in their tracks. How? Be a good egg: Never buy tortoiseshell jewelry or items made from other endangered species. Enjoy nature naturally, in the wild, instead!

Q. Where have all the frogs gone?

A. That is what scientists around the world are wondering. They say that they are seeing fewer amphibians, such as frogs, toads, and salamanders. Since amphibians have been around for some 350 million years, that is a big deal!

What does the decline in the number of amphibians mean for humans? Some amphibians, such as frogs, are called *indicator species*. This means that they are the first animals to be affected when something is wrong in their environment. So when amphibians start showing signs of stress—such as the frog at right, which has a deformed leg—scientists pay attention to how that environment is affecting people.

Q. When is water not all wet?

A. When it appears as ice or water vapor. Our planet reuses the same water all the time, in the water cycle. Water evaporates from lakes, rivers, and oceans, and becomes water vapor in the atmosphere. Eventually it condenses and becomes part of a cloud. When the clouds get loaded with water, they release it as precipitation—rain, snow, sleet, or hail. The water falls to the ground and ends up back in the lakes, rivers, and oceans. Then the water cycle repeats itself.

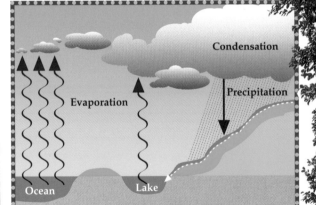

Q. Do trees ever drink water through a straw?

A. Well, sort of. The roots of a tree act like a straw by sucking up water from the ground. When it rains, water falls and is soaked up by the soil. The roots of a tree, which spread out as far below ground as the branches spread above, seek out that water. Defying gravity, the water travels up the trunk, through the branches, and finally into the leaves. If the water the tree drinks is polluted, the tree will suffer.

Q. When is it a bad idea to go with the flow?

When you're brushing your teeth, taking a shower, or washing the car. On average, each person uses about 168 gallons of water a day! That is a lot of water.

So how can people around the world conserve water? By taking shorter showers, for one thing, or turning off the faucet while you brush your teeth or do the dishes. You can also ask your parents to install a low-flow showerhead and a "toilet dam" in the bathroom. These save water and money. Finally, be sure to repair leaky faucets. A leaky faucet can waste up to 1,000 gallons of water a year!

Q. Can trout be burned by a raindrop?

Not literally, but fish and other living things do get "burned" by acid rain all the time. Acid rain forms when clean rainwater gets contaminated by sulfur dioxide and ozone in polluted air. When too much of this polluted rainwater lands in a pond, lake, river, or ocean, wildlife in the water suffers.

If you ever see a body of water that looks too clean, you had better worry. Very clear water could be a sign that acid rain has killed off all the fish, plants, algae, and other organisms that used to live there.

Q. When is a mailbox like a garbage dump?

A. When it is filled with junk mail. Did you ever take a close look at your mail? You'll probably see a lot that you don't need, such as catalogs and flyers. If you saved all of your junk mail for one year, you would have the equivalent of one and a half trees! If everyone in the U. S. saved all their junk mail, it would equal 100 million trees each year! How can we save all those trees from being wasted? Recycle any junk mail you have. Also, send a letter to *Mail Preference Service, P.O. Box 9008, Farmingdale, NY, 11735-9008*, requesting that your name and address be removed from advertisers' mailing lists.

A. Don't worry. If you do buy the same thing twice, you are not necessarily being ripped off. A can of soda that you buy today can be recycled and back on the store shelf, refilled, in 60 days. That is a good thing—especially since the average American drinks at least one can of soda a day! Aluminum cans are a recycling success story. For one thing, aluminum can be recycled again and again without falling apart. In the U.S., about 527,000 aluminum cans are recycled each minute! That is almost 64 billion cans a year.

Q. Do recycled newspapers make good homes?

A. Yes! As a matter of fact, about 1.5 million tons of construction products are made out of recycled paper each year. Paper is used to make wallboards, roofing paper, ceiling tiles, and building insulation. Since paper can't be recycled over and over again the way aluminum and glass can, it makes sense to use it in building materials where it can stay a long time.

In 1993, for the first time in U.S. history, more paper was recovered for reuse than wound up at the city dump. That means that fewer trees were being chopped down!

Q. How can a soda bottle keep me warm on a camping trip?

A. By filling up your sleeping bag. No, not with soda, with recycled plastic! When plastic soft-drink bottles are recycled, they are sometimes chopped up, melted down, and stuffed into parkas and sleeping bags as insulation, to keep users warm. More and more companies are finding unusual uses for recycled products. Old polystyrene containers are refashioned into cassette boxes and yo-yos. As for old newspapers, besides becoming yesterday's news, they also make perfect egg cartons and cereal boxes.

Q. Why do green plants make great chefs?

A. Because they make their own food in a process called photosynthesis. They start with sunlight, water, and carbon dioxide from the air. Using the energy from the sun and the chlorophyll in their leaves, plants use these ingredients to make carbohydrates. They use the carbohydrates for energy to survive. When plants are done "cooking," they release oxygen gas into the atmosphere. Without green plants, we would not have food to eat or oxygen to breathe.

Q. Would a flower ever tell a bee to buzz off? zᶻᶻᶻᶻᶻᶻ

A. No way! Flowers need bees just as much as bees need flowers. They help each other all the time. Flowers use their sweet-smelling nectar and pretty colors to lure bees. For bees, nectar and pollen are nutritious, loaded with protein, vitamins, and carbohydrates. As the bees dive in, however, they are doing the flowers a favor, too. At each stop a bee makes, pollen sticks to its body *(left)*. As the bee goes from flower to flower, it keeps picking up and dropping off pollen. This process, called pollination, helps new flower seeds grow.

Q. Do russet Burbanks make good couch potatoes?

A. No—but they do make good french fries! Russet Burbanks (also called Idaho potatoes) are among the hundreds of varieties of potatoes grown in the world today. Yet, with all these spuds on the planet, only a dozen or so types make it to most supermarket shelves. Why? Large commercial farms with modern equipment find it cheaper to plant *monocultures*—large tracts of land growing only one crop. But some farmers prefer variety among their crops. Some even grow "heirloom" fruits and vegetables, which were cultivated by past generations. Some organizations try to preserve such rare "heirlooms" by collecting their seeds from around the world.

Q. When do plants make great pioneers?

A. When they are lichens (LY-kinz)! Lichens—a combination of a fungus and an algae—are among the oldest living things in nature. They can live for hundreds, even thousands, of years. Lichens grow almost everywhere in the world, including the North and South poles. They are commonly found on rocks (*left*), logs, and tree bark. Lichens are also likely to be the first things to grow back in an area after a volcano erupts. Because they can grow in harsh conditions, lichens prepare the way for less rugged species to follow.

What are these adventurers of the plant kingdom used for? Drug companies make antibiotics from them. They are also a great source of food for caribou and other such creatures.

Q. Do prairie dogs and beavers need hardware stores?

A. No; both carry their own built-in tools. Beavers *(left)* gnaw through trees with their tough front teeth to build dams in streams. Prairie dogs *(below)* use the claws on their forefeet to dig underground homes. But dig this: The homes that these creatures build also help the environment! A prairie dog's burrowing is good for the soil. The tunnels also make great homes for other animals, such as owls, badgers, and rabbits. Beaver dams keep water at a comfortable depth for fish and the birds that feed on them. Dams also help prevent soil erosion near the shore.

Q. Could old McDonald's farm ever leave him high and dry?

A. Yes, if he isn't careful about soil erosion. Soil erosion is what happens when layers of soil are blown or washed away by wind, water, or improper care. When this happens, crops can't grow. That leads to trouble for old McDonald and other farmworkers.

Soil is always eroding. Even mountain ranges wear down after millions of years. But erosion occurs more quickly when natural disasters take place. Sometimes, people cause erosion by cutting down too many trees or overfarming. In the 1930s, soil erosion was a big problem in North America's Great Plains. A drought and strong winds caused huge quantities of dry soil to blow away. The area *(right)* became known as the Dust Bowl.

Q. What grows on a hazmat?

A. Hopefully, nothing. *Hazmat* is short for "hazardous materials." Hazmats are created as waste products during the manufacture of many of today's products, such as toys, clothes, computers, and cars. Some household items—such as old paint cans, batteries, used motor oil, and weed killers—are also considered hazmats.

Until the 1970s, hazmats were buried. These substances leaked from rusty barrels *(right)* and seeped into the soil and underground water supply. As a result, many people got sick. Today, environmentalists and lawmakers are looking for better ways to dispose of hazmats, so that soil and water stay clean. You can call your city or county government office to find out how to properly dispose of any hazmats you may have at your home.

Q. Why do farmers make good COACHES?

A. They know when to rotate their players! Farmland, like athletes, needs rest. By rotating crops, farmers give the soil a rest.

Some crops, such as cotton, pound the soil by taking nitrates and other nutrients from it. When a different crop, such as peanuts or other legumes, are planted in the same soil, different nutrients are used and others are replaced. Alternating cotton with legumes makes the soil healthier. That is why, in the late 1800s, an agricultural scientist named George Washington Carver recommended that farmers vary the crops they grow. Today, most farmers do.

Q. On what kind of grass do humans graze?

A. Rice, wheat, corn, oats, rye, and barley. These are all different forms of grass. Grasses grow across the globe, from the Arctic tundra to the southern tips of the continents. Grass is one of the most common types of plants in the world.

Like other natural habitats, large grasslands are home to a wide variety of plants and animals. Bison *(below)*, deer, and rabbits, for example, all graze on grasslands. When people plow these areas—or use them to feed farm animals, such as cattle, sheep, and horses—other species in the environment, such as insects and birds, suffer.

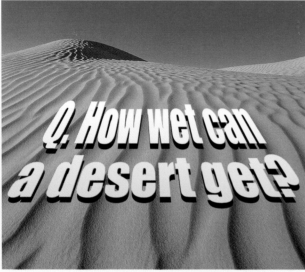

Q. How wet can a desert get?

A. Very wet, say most experts. Thousands of years ago, even the African Sahara—the largest desert in the world—was filled with green grasses and low shrubs, all of which were nourished by rainwater.

What happened? Desertification! It happens all over the world in various ways. Sometimes, winds blow sand from dune areas to duneless ones. People contribute to the process, too, when they chop down too many trees or try to cultivate poor soil.

The Sahara, in large part, was formed another way. Over time, the tilt of Earth and its orbit have gradually changed. This led to new weather patterns, which caused less rain to fall over the Sahara.

A. One reason is the rain forest's temperature, which is about 80°F day and night, all year. But it is also because much of their habitat is being burned to make way for farms.

Q. Why are creatures of the rain forest getting hot under the collar?

Each tree in a rain forest is an entire community in itself. Every time one comes down, many plants and animals (such as the orangutan below) lose their home. Some experts estimate that 100 acres of rain forest are burned down every minute. However, most rain forest nutrients are in the trees, so the soil underneath makes poor farmland.

Q. Do birds flying south ever stay at the Dew Drop Inn?

A. No, but they may stop off at a wetland or two along the way. Wetlands are soggy habitats—such as bogs, swamps, and marshes—that contain a lot of moisture in the soil. For a long time, no one understood the importance of wetlands.

Farmers would drain or fill up these areas to grow crops. Other people would build homes or even cities, like Boston and Washington, D.C. Now, however, people are starting to recognize the importance of wetlands. Besides making great rest stops for migrating birds, wetlands soak up water when there is a flood, and act as safe havens for many animal species.

Q. Do snakes wear sunscreen?

A Not really, but all living things on Earth are protected from the sun by the ozone layer, a section of Earth's atmosphere, 12 to 30 miles above the planet. It is made up of ozone—a type of oxygen gas—which helps protect all living things from the sun's ultraviolet (UV) rays.

In exchange for its protection of us, it is our job to protect the ozone layer. Thinning areas of ozone have been spotted above the North and South poles, as you can see by the dark blue area above Antarctica, shown at right. That is why, by 1998, 150 countries signed an agreement to stop producing ozone-destroying chemicals called chlorofluorocarbons (KLOR-oh-FLOR-oh KAR-bunz), or CFCs. CFCs were once used in air conditioners, refrigerators, spray cans, and foam packaging materials. Today, their production has largely stopped.

Q. Do buildings ever get sick?

A. Yes. A building may be suspected of having *sick-building syndrome* (SBS) when many of the people in it start feeling ill at the same time. Symptoms of SBS include headaches; eye, nose, or throat irritation; nausea; itchy skin; and fatigue. Sufferers often feel better soon after they get outside.

SBS buildings usually have poor air circulation. Even worse, irritating chemicals have sometimes become trapped in the air supply. To make the building well, experts must find the problem, then correct it.

Q. Am I getting *zapped* by my microwave oven?

A. Scientists don't think so. Some people, though, worry about microwave cooking because they think that radiation is being used to heat the food. Microwaves are short waves of electromagnetic energy that travel at the speed of light. Just about all American homes and restaurants have microwave ovens. So far, studies show that they are safe.

Q. Could I get bitten by a peach?

A. Yes, if it has been sprayed with pesticides! Pesticides are substances that protect crops from bugs, weeds, and rodents. They also keep bathrooms free of mold and mildew, and keep fleas off your pets. If they are used improperly, however, pesticides can harm the environment and you, too.

The U.S. government and some others limit the amount of pesticides that can wind up on fruits and veggies. To get rid of the rest, always wash produce before you eat it. You might also suggest that your parents buy organically grown products. This means they were made or grown without pesticides.

Q. When does a six-pack of soda pack a mean punch?

A. When birds and other animals get caught in the plastic rings that hold the cans together. When animals get trapped in the plastic rings, they can be strangled by the plastic, or die from starvation because they can't get food. You can help: Whenever you see a six-pack ring, cut all the loops apart, then recycle it.

Six-pack rings were first created to *help* the environment, not hurt it: They use less plastic than other forms of packaging. However, it still takes 10 or more years for the material in the rings to decay.

Q. Who are the big fish in the sea these days?

A. The small fry, that's who! In general, the average size of fish is getting smaller. Folks who go fishing are always on the lookout for the biggest fish they can catch. That leaves a lot of lightweights to breed future generations. So the catch of the day is shrinking each year.

In recent years, environmentalists have been asking seafood lovers to give big fish a break. Restaurants are trying to help by taking such dishes as Atlantic salmon, swordfish, Chilean sea bass, and shark off the menu.

Q. What gives a penguin the shivers?

A. An oil spill—like the one that took place in Alaska's Prince William Sound in 1989. Not only do oil spills pollute the water, but slick, black oil also mats the fur of sea animals, such as penguins *(right)* and otters. This leaves them with little protection from the cold. To get rid of the oil, otters try to lick it off themselves. But then they swallow the oil, which is poisonous.

How can you help otters and penguins? By walking or riding your bike instead of driving in a car. Most oil is used for gasoline. The less oil people use, the less oil needs to be transported, which lessens the chance of an oil spill at sea.

Q. WHAT ARE 25 MILLION YEARS OLD AND STILL GROWING?

A. Some coral reefs. Coral reefs can be found in warm, shallow parts of the ocean. They are home to countless life forms. Coral reefs *(below)* are made up of tiny living things called polyps. Polyps secrete the hard material that forms the skeleton of the reef. Because of this, the reef itself is considered a living thing.

Like other undersea life, coral reefs thrive in clean water. Pollution and overfishing are causing a lot of damage. Today, people are taking steps to protect coral reefs. In the meantime, old ships, planes, and other debris sometimes serve as artificial reefs. They give algae, sea sponges, and coral a new place to build their homes.

The largest coral reef in the world, the Great Barrier Reef in Australia, is more than 1,200 miles long.

Q. What is the coolest protected land on Earth?

A. Antarctica! That's right: The fifth-largest continent, and the coldest place on the planet, is now a protected land. It also is one of the cleanest places on Earth. In 1991, the Protocol on Environmental Protection was added to the Antarctic Treaty (an agreement developed in 1959 and signed by more than 25 countries). The Protocol on Environmental Protection will protect the environment of Antarctica for the next 50 years. No company or government can dig for oil, minerals, or other resources until 2038. The penguins, seals, and whales that live there and in the oceans around it are probably safe for now. So is two thirds of the Earth's fresh water supply, and almost all of the ice on Earth.

Q. WHEN WERE ANIMALS CAGED LIKE CRIMINALS?

A. In early zoos. The first zoos were not much more than cages in a park. The animals had little room to exercise and play. Modern zoos, however, work hard to imitate natural settings and create healthy environments for all the animals there.

Zoos educate people on the importance of wildlife. They also play a role in conservation. Many large zoos in the U.S. adopt parks in poorer parts of the world. Many zoos also protect and try to breed animals that can no longer survive in the wild, like the giant panda *(left)*. If not for zoos, endangered species, such as the California condor, might be extinct.

Q. Does anyone give a hoot about the northern spotted owl?

A. They sure do. For more than a decade, environmentalists and loggers in California, Oregon, and Washington have been at odds over this endangered bird. Northern spotted owls thrive in old-growth forests, where loggers often work. When loggers cut trees for lumber and to open an area for roads, the owls suffer. But if the loggers leave the forests alone, they will lose their jobs.

In 1994, loggers and owl fans reached a compromise. Loggers can cut trees in forests that are less than 80 years old, but must leave older trees—where most of the owls live—alone. They also have to plant new trees.

Q. When is it great to turn green?

A. Any time! To environmentalists, "being green" means taking care of the planet in everything you do. Whenever you reduce, reuse, or recycle—or encourage others to do it—you are being green. This book shows you lots of ways to do just that. The more you work at being green, the greener you become. Planet Earth needs government agencies, large corporations, and organizations to be green as well. If everybody pitches in, Earth will be a cleaner, greener place for plants and animals alike.

Glossary

Acid rain: Rain that has been contaminated by chemicals in the air.

Atmosphere: The gases that surround Earth.

Biodegradable: Something that breaks down into harmless substances over time.

Carbon dioxide: A gas in the atmosphere that green plants use to make food. Carbon dioxide also traps heat. It is considered a greenhouse gas.

Compost: Organic trash—such as egg shells, banana peels, and orange rinds—that is used to fertilize soil.

Endangered species: Plants or animals that are at risk of becoming extinct.

Extinct: No longer existing.

Fluorescent light: An energy-saving form of electric light.

Fossil fuels: Materials derived from dead plant and animal matter, such as natural gas, oil, and coal.

Greenhouse effect: When warm air gets trapped in the atmosphere by greenhouse gases, such as carbon dioxide.

Hazmat: Harmful waste products. *Hazmat* is short for hazardous material.

Incandescent light: A form of electric light invented by Thomas Edison. Incandescent light is not very efficient, because it produces more heat than light.

Landfill: A large area where garbage trucks dump trash.

Nuclear power: Electricity that is generated by nuclear reactions.

Ozone layer: A layer of gas high in the atmosphere that protects Earth from the sun's damaging rays.

Photosynthesis: The process by which plants use sunlight, carbon dioxide, and chlorophyll (in their leaves) to make food.

Poaching: The killing or capturing of plants or animals (including eggs) that are protected by law.

Pollution: Contamination of air, water, or soil with human-made waste.

Polystyrene: The general name for plastic packing material; also known as Styrofoam.

Radiation: Energy released by certain substances, such as radioactive elements, in the form of waves or particles.

Recycle: To reuse.

Soil erosion: The washing away of soil by water, wind, or human abuse.